GERMAN SITES
IN LONDON

A pictorial guide

Edited by
Rolf Breitenstein and
Angelika Hommerich

OSWALD WOLFF

in co-operation with the
Embassy of the Federal Republic of Germany
London

© 1976 Oswald Wolff (Publishers) Limited, London W1M 6DR
Jacket design by Felix Mussil
ISBN 0 85496 207 7

Printed in Great Britain by
Kingprint Limited,
Richmond, Surrey.

IN THIS BOOK

About 100,000 Germans live in Great Britain. 30,000 of them live in Greater London — or possibly 25,841 or 34,127. Nobody knows the precise figure. They are businessmen and journalists, technicians and students, chefs in hotels and workers in factories, wives and children of British husbands and fathers. They are registered nowhere and they don't live clustered together. London has its Chinatown, but no German-town. There are old historical sights like the churches and new building sites for the German School and for the Goethe Institute, but the many-sided German community is scattered all over London. If those Germans were asked to name a rallying point, most of them would hesitate and then suggest the *Embassy in Belgrave Square*. Therefore — after a glimpse at some *1881 vintage advertisements* on the opposite page — in this pictorial guide the Embassy, the old Legal and Consular Department and the building site for the new one, and the five Ambassadors who have served here after the war, are introduced first. Then the camera is quickly turned to the many varied facets of things German in London.

GERMAN POST-WAR AMBASSADORS TO LONDON

Hans Schlange-Schöningen
(1950-1955)

Hans-Heinrich Herwarth
von Bittenfeld (1955-1961)

Hasso von Etzdorf
(1961-1965)

Herbert Blankenhorn
(1965-1970)

Karl-Günther von Hase
Ambassador of the Federal Republic
of Germany (since 1970)

3

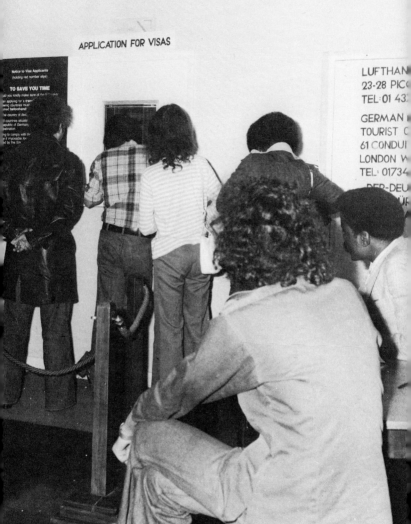

APPLICATION FOR VISAS

FEDERAL REPUBLIC OF GERMANY

utschland

Erweiterungsbau
Represented by
Vertreten durch Bundesbaudirektion

hitekten BDA

cts, planners
Wimslow

m

dshire

architect

MAIN CONTRACTORS

TTC Trollope & Colls Ltd.

SUB CONTRACTORS & SUPPLIERS

TROLLOPE & COLLS LTD
APOLOGISE FOR ANY INCONVENIENCE
CAUSED BY THIS DEVELOPMENT

CHESHAM
PLACE SW1
CITY OF WESTMINSTER

6

Under a mighty tree in Carlton House Terrace, about half way between the house where General de Gaulle resided in the last war and the "citadel" built by the Admiralty in the Mall, there stands a simple stone bearing the inscription: *"Giro — ein treuer Begleiter"* (Giro — a faithful companion). The stone has jolted into action a number of English and German journalists who happened to discover it and began to speculate: A German agent buried by a friend? Not at all. The stone marks one of those German mysteries which are easy to unravel: The burial of a dog who, when alive, belonged to German Ambassador von Hoesch. The Ambassador resided in the old German Embassy nearby.

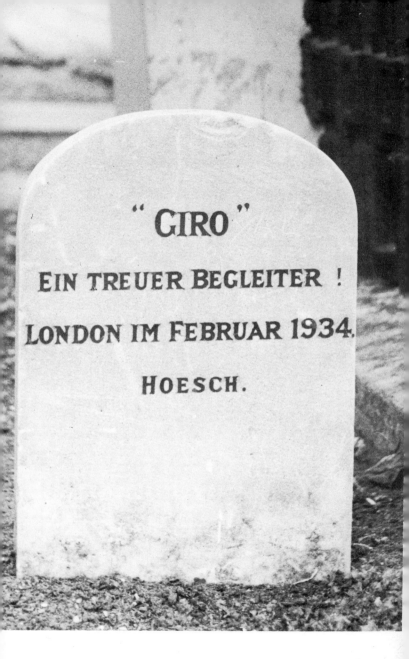

"GIRO"

EIN TREUER BEGLEITER !

LONDON IM FEBRUAR 1934.

HOESCH.

The *German Deaconess and Guest Home* (p.13) was founded in 1930 as a hostel for those training to be missionaries. They came to England to learn the language. Like some other German institutions it has over the years outgrown its original purpose: Nowadays most German school-children learn to speak English well enough to get by. The German hostel has been turned into an international one, although Germans and particularly future missionaries are still given preference. Similarly the *German Hospital* (p.11) changed from a German foundation into a National Health hospital. The *German Welfare Council* (p.12) was set up in 1952, when a great number of Germans who had come to Britain during or after the war, faced social problems. The Council's social work ranges from legal aid to group meetings with German pensioners. Young people who work in London as au pairs are looked after by the *Verein für Internationale Jugendarbeit* (p. 14). And the *German Seemannsheim* (p.15) arranges film shows, sightseeing tours, and lectures for German sailors who come to the London docks. The *Old People's Home* (pp.16/17), which has been in South London in its present form since 1966, has room for 27 people. Medical care is provided by Croydon Council.

11

13

The *German YMCA* (p.19) is a community centre for German families who have made their home in London, and also for young people who are working or studying in London. There is an 'Anglo-German-Circle' which meets once a week, and once a month older German people get together. The YMCA also maintains a counselling service. In the German YMCA hostel there are 200 beds: 50 of these are available cheaply to school parties or students. The German Young Men's Christian Association was founded in 1860 by a group of young Germans who had come to London to work in hotels, restaurants and delicatessen stores.

Rebuilding at the *Goethe-Instiute* (p.21) began in July 1975. In spite of the inconvenience, the Institute continued its services as comprehensively as ever. The Goethe-Institute, whose headquarters are in Munich and which has 113 branches all over the world, is responsible for the promotion of German language teaching and culture abroad. The London Institute runs language classes (p.22) for about 400 people per year and maintains a library which, in 1972, was the venue of a "promenade concert" (p.24). The most ambitious event so far arranged jointly by the London Institute and the Arts Council was the 'German Month' in the autumn of 1974 which drew over 180,000 visitors. One of its highlights was the first English language performance of 'The Highwaymen' ('Die Räuber') by Friedrich von Schiller (p.23).

21

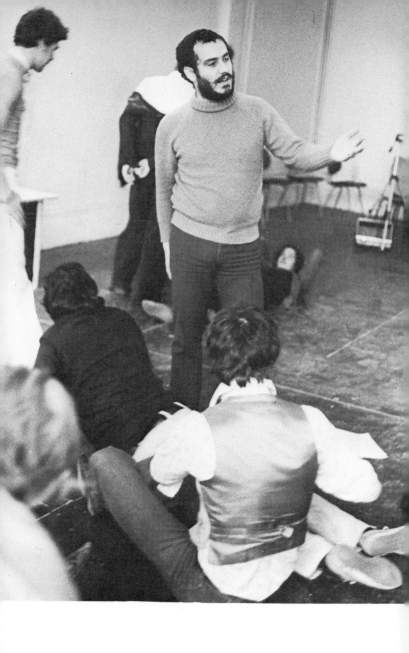

The *German School, London*, which was founded in Richmond in 1971, soon outgrew its original space. The school is built around a beautiful manor house (pp.26/27), which is now used by the school administration. The temporary facilities of the school's early years are being replaced by a modern school building with classrooms, a gymnasium and swimming pool (model p.28). The new buildings can accommodate 650 pupils. These are mainly children from families who stay in London only for a few years. A regular bus service takes the children from various parts of London to Richmond in the morning and brings them back again in the late afternoon.

DEUTSCHE SCHULE
LONDON

SCALE 1:500

In 1975 the Federal Republic of Germany was Britain's second largest trading partner — 6.4% of all British exports went to the Federal Republic and 8.3% of all goods imported to Britain came from Germany. In addition to the Embassy's Commercial Section, the *German Chamber of Industry and Commerce* (p.30) helps to strengthen the trading links by giving market information to British and German exporters. The Chamber also arranges regional visits and seminars both in Germany and in Britain. For many years the *Bundesverband der deutschen Industrie* (BDI) had an office in Bruton Street (p.31) which also gave trade information, maintained contacts with its opposite number, the CBI, and held monthly meetings for German firms in Britain. In October 1976 the office was transferred to the premises of the German Chamber of Industry and Commerce.

31

The *German Food Centre* in Knightsbridge (p.33) is crammed with samples of the great variety of German food exported to Britain — from Pumpernickel and Leberwurst to 'Hock' and 'Schnapps'. It serves a double purpose — to whet the appetite of Britain's shopkeepers for German fare, and as a last resort for expatriate German housewives desparate for their 'vanilla sugar' and 'Götterspeise'. Food for thought, on the other hand, can be found in the *German Historical Institute* (pp.34,35). Its library facilities mainly serve British historians interested in German history. The Institute, officially opened in November 1976, is already looking for more shelf-space.

Spurred by their studies, many young Germans and Britons want to go on exchange visits. Through scholarships, the *German Academic Exchange Service* (DAAD) (pp.37,38) has helped many of them to carry out their plans. There are several other institutions, which, like the German Academic Exchange Service, contribute to mutual understanding and information. The *Anglo-German-Association* (p.39), founded in 1951, is one of them. Through its youth organisation and its Anglo-German Clubs in the provinces it has brought about a host of personal links between Britons and Germans.

On 12 April, 1826, the German composer Carl Maria von Weber (1786 — 1826) conducted the first performance of his last opera *'Oberon'* at the Theatre Royal, Covent Garden (p.41). Weber's journey to London in 1826 was his only trip to England. He died on 4 July 1826 at Ian Smart's, his host's house in Great Portland Street. 'Oberon' was a great success in London, but Weber's most famous opera is probably 'Der Freischütz', which he composed in 1820.

NEVER ACTED.

Theatre Royal, Covent-Garden,

This present **WEDNESDAY**, April 12, 1826,

Will be performed *(for the first time)* a Grand Romantic and Fairy Opera, in three acts, (Founded on Wieland's celebrated Poem) entitled

OBERON:

OR,

THE ELF-KING's OATH.

With entirely new Music, Scenery, Machinery, Dresses and Decorations.

The OVERTURE and the whole of the MUSIC composed by

CARL MARIA VON WEBER,

Who will preside this Evening in the Orchestra.

The CHORUS (under the direction of Mr. WATSON,) has been greatly augmented.
The DANCES composed by Mr. AUSTIN.
The Scenes painted by Mess. GRIEVE, PUGH, T. and W. GRIEVE, LUPPINO, and assistants.
The Machinery by Mr. E. SAUL. The Aerial Machinery, Transformations & Decorations by Mess. BRADWELL
The Dresses by Mr. PALMER, Miss EGAN, and assistants.

Fairies.

Oberon, *King of the Fairies*, Mr. C. BLAND, Puck, Miss H. CAWSE,
Titania, *Queen of the Fairies*, Miss SMITH.

*The Mermaid Ltd by
Miss Goward*

Franks.

Charlemagne, *King of the Franks*, Mr. AUSTIN,
Sir Huon, of Bourdeaux, *Duke of Guienne*,..............Mr. BRAHAM,
Sherasmin, *his Squire*,................Mr. FAWCETT.

Arabians.

Haroun-Al-Raschid, *Caliph of Bagdad*, Mr. CHAPMAN,
Baba Khan, *a Saracenic Prince*, Mr. BAKER, Hassan, *Master of a Vessel*, Mr. J. ISAACS,
Hamet, Mr. EVANS, Amrou, M. ATKINS,
Reiza, *Daughter of the Caliph*,............Miss PATON,
Fatima, Madame VESTRIS,
Namouna, *Fatima's Grandmother*, Mrs. DAVENPORT.

Tunisians.

Almanzor, *Emir of Tunis*,......Mr. COOPER,
Aboalfh, *a Corsair*, Mr. HORREBOW, Slave, Mr. TINNEY,
Roshana, *Wife of Almanzor*,............Miss LACY,
Sadina, *a female Slave*, Mrs. WILSON,
Officers, Soldiers, Slaves, &c. of the different Courts,——Fairies, Sprites, &c.

Order of the Scenery:

OBERON'S BOWER,

With the VISION. Painted by Mr. Grieve.
Distant View of Bagdad, and the adjacent Country on the Banks of the Tigris,
By Samert. Grieve.
INTERIOR of NAMOUNA's COTTAGE, T. Grieve
VESTIBULE and TERRACE in the HAREM of the CALIPH, overlooking the Tigris, W. Grieve
GRAND BANQUETTING CHAMBER of HAROUN, T. Grieve.
GARDENS of the PALACE. Pugh
PORT OF ASCALON. T. Grieve
RAVINE amongst the ROCKS of a DESOLATE ISLAND,
The Haunt of the Spirits of the Storm. Designed by Bradwell, and painted by Pugh.

Perforated Cavern on the Beach,

With the OCEAN—in a STORM—a CALM—by SUNSET—
Twilight—Starlight—and Moonlight. T. Grieve
Exterior of Gardener's House in the Pleasure Grounds of the Emir of Tunis. Grieve
Hall and Gallery in Almansor's Palace. W. Grieve
MYRTLE GROVE in the GARDENS of the EMIR. Pugh
GOLDEN SALOON in the KIOSK of ROSHANA. W. Grieve.
The Palace and Gardens, by Moonlight. Grieve.
COURT of the HAREM. Pugh.
HALL of ARMS in the Palace of Charlemagne. Grieve & Luppino

The Opera is published, & may be had in the Theatre, & of Mess. Hunt & Clarke, 38, Tavistock-street, Covent-garden

To which will be added (23d time) a NEW PIECE, in one act, called

THE SCAPE-GOAT.

Old Eustace, Mr. BLANCHARD, Charles, Mr. COOPER,
Ignatius Polyglot, Mr. W. FARREN, Robin, Mr. MEADOWS,
Molly Maggs, Miss JONES, Harriet, Miss A. JONES.

W. REYNOLDS, Printer, 9. Denmark-Court, Strand.

The services in the German churches in London are often held in both English and German for the benefit of the English husbands, wives and children of German nationals. Many of the German wives got married to their British husbands while these were serving in the British Army on the Rhine. Many of the other male worshippers are former POWs who stayed on, or refugees who came to Britain in the 1930s. The *Deutsche Evangelische Christuskirche* (pp.43,44,45) was built in 1904 after the Königlich Deutsche Hofkapelle in St. James Palace was closed in 1902 by King Edward VII. Count Henry von Schröder then decided that the parish should not be without a church and had the Christuskirche built.

45

The Roman Catholic *St. Boniface's Church* (pp.47,48) was opened in 1960 and has been the meeting place for many Germans in London ever since. St. Boniface's modern parish centre Wynfrid House was built ten years later and contains besides community rooms a number of guest rooms. Visitors staying at Wynfrid House can also get their meals there. The *German Catholic Social Centre St. Lioba* (p.49) particularly serves German au pairs who work in London. The German Centre functions as an agency for au pairs, organises a cultural programme and many special events and also runs a small hostel.

Dietrich Bonhoeffer, one of the most outstanding theologians of the 20th century, was hanged by the Nazis in 1945. From 1933–1935 he served as minister to the German parishes of Sydenham and St. Paul. This was the only post he held as a pastor before turning to teaching. He belonged to the 'Confessional Church', the anti-Nazi opposition within the church. By 1940 he and many of his friends and relatives were involved in underground political activities aimed at the assassination of Hitler and the overthrow of the Nazi regime. The new parish church in South London, opened in 1959 (pp.51,52), was named after Dietrich Bonhoeffer, who used to live nearby (p.53).

Between the old houses in Sandwich Street, London W.C.1, a modern building emerges: a Lutheran Student Centre on the site of the *St. Marienkirche* (p.55). There will be a hostel for 85 students, mainly from Commonwealth countries, and the St. Marienkirche itself will be housed in the basement and on the ground floor. The Church will thus be available to the students at all times. The St. Marienkirche, which was founded in 1694, is one of the oldest German churches in London.

The *St. Georgskirche* (pp.57), which was opened in 1763, is the only German Church in London, which has survived in its original building. The *Hamburger Lutherische Kirche* (pp.58,59) is the oldest Lutheran Church in London and like many others was moved from one place to another. The Hamburg Lutheran Church was founded in 1669 by foreign craftsmen and merchants who had been asked by Charles II to come to London to help rebuild the city after the Great Fire. The present Church in Dalston was built next to the German hospital, after its former site was taken over by the London underground.

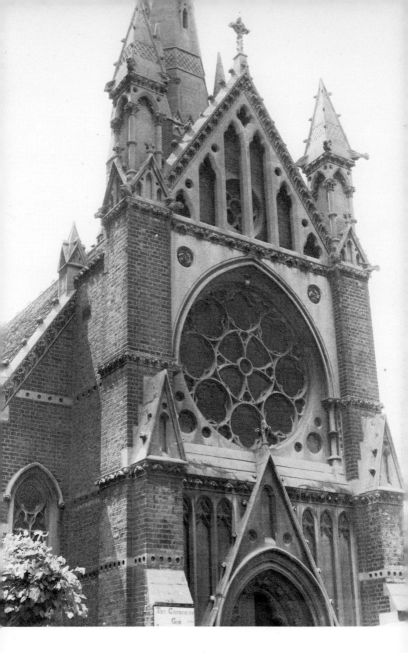

Payment is usually accepted in German currency only (15,00 DM per head) at the *Peter Boehler House* (p.61) just off King's Cross. This hostel belongs to the *German Methodist Mission*, which is over a hundred years old and had, until 1971, a mission house in Drayton Park. In 1973 the German Methodist Mission joined with the English Methodist Church in King's Cross. The German Mission still cares mainly for Germans: Au pairs find help, and there are regular meetings at weekends and other special events (p.62).

GERMAN METHODIST MISSION
DEUTSCHE MISSION

WELCOME TO OUR
SUNDAY SERVICES

11 a.m.
ENGLISH SERVICE and SUNDAY SCHOOL
(Family Service on 3rd Sunday)
5 p.m.
ANGLO·GERMAN SERVICE
(Bi·lingual)
6 p.m.
FELLOWSHIP TEA
Entrance in Crestfield Street.

In 1975 the total of about 1.2 million overnight stays by Britons in the Federal Republic of Germany was up by six per cent on the previous year. Several institutions in London promote travel to Germany: *Lufthansa* (pp.64, 65) runs 16 flights a day from London to German cities. *German Tourist Facilities* (pp.66, 67) specialize in Charter flights to Germany. The London office of the *German Federal Railway* (p.68) advertises travel by railway to, from and inside Germany and organises freight traffic. The *DER* (p.69), largest Travel Organization in Germany, specializes in booking individual and group travel to Germany.

German Tourist Facilities Ltd

01-229-9427

TOURIST INFORMATION
TOURISTENBERATUNG

SIGHTSEEING TOURS
STADTRUNDFAHRTEN

CAR HIRE
LEIHWAGEN

HOTEL BOOKINGS
HOTELBUCHUNGEN

THEATRE TICKETS
THEATERKARTEN

FLIGHT INSURANCE
FLUGVERSICHERUNGEN

CHARTER FLIGHTS
ONDON·GERMANY·LONDON
CHARTER FLÜGE

The *German National Tourist Office* in London (p.71) is one of the 16 foreign branches of the "Deutsche Zentrale für Tourismus", subsidised by the Federal Government. Its main objective is to carry out publicity for the Federal Republic of Germany and to co-operate with other national and international authorities. Student travel is promoted by the *German Student Travel Service* (pp.72, 73): At present, every year about 3,500 students go to Germany by air, 20,000 go by train and another 5,000 young people travel as members of parties. Britons who wish to visit Baden-Baden, one of many German spas, can book at the *Baden-Baden Tourist Office* (p.74).

NATIONAL TOURIST OFFICE

GERMANY

THE COUNTRY TO

Germany - Land of Variety,
Land of Contrasts!

Why not do your discovering with us,
we are at home over there. We
have the best connections in and
around Germany as well as the best
information about our homeland.
Go ahead and consult us - right
here, and discover a Germany that
has more to offer than sauerkraut,
pretzels and leather breeches.

Photo Index

Photos by K. Fields (unless otherwise credited)

62	German Methodist Mission (58, Birkenhead Street, London WC1, Tel. 01-837 4518)
64	Offices of German Federal Railway and Lufthansa, (10, Old Bond Street, London W1)
65	Lufthansa Office, (23/28 Piccadilly, London W1, Tel. 01-437 0434)
66	German Tourist Facilities (184, Kensington Church Street, London W8, Tel. 01-229 9427)
67	Posters at German Tourist Facilities
68	Office of German Federal Railway (10, Old Bond Street, London W1, Tel. 01-499 0577/8/9)
69	DER-Travel Service (16-17 Orchard Street, London W1, Tel. 01-486 4593)
71	German National Tourist Office (61, Conduit Street, London W1, Tel. 01-734 2600)
72	German Student Travel Service (Terminal House, 52 Grosvenor Gardens, Lower Belgrave Street, London SW1, Tel. 01-730 2101)
73	At the German Student Travel Service
74	Baden-Baden Tourist Authority (6/8, Old Bond Street, London W1, Tel. 01-493 5878)

ANGLO-GERMAN RELATIONS

Other books published in co-operation with the London Embassy of the Federal Republic of Germany.

Forthcoming
Total War to Total Trust

Personal accounts of 30 years of Anglo-German relations—the vital role of non-governmental organisations.

Edited by Rolf Breitenstein.

Introduced by Lothar Kettenacker

Contents :
Inside Featherstone Park, by Herbert Sulzbach
The Anglo-German Association, by George Turner, M.B.E.
The Anglo-German Parliamentary Group, by Sir Bernard Braine, M.P.
The Anglo-German Foundation for the Study of Industrial Society, by Peter McGregor

0 85496 208 5   *Crown 8vo, 104 pp., limp binding* £2.75

A second volume is planned for 1977—with contributions expected to range from the BBC German Service to the Koenigswinter Conference.

Previously Published
Twinning

DEUTSCH-BRITISCHE PARTNERSCHAFTEN

Foreword by H.E. *The Ambassador of the Federal Republic of Germany*
Afterthoughts by George Mikes

Reports, documents and photographs illustrating the exchange between towns and regions in Britain and the Federal Republic of Germany.

0 85496 202 6   *Crown 8vo, 164 pp., fully illus., index, cloth* £2.50

Boys & Girls & Germany

Edited by Rolf Breitenstein and Angelika Hommerich

The Federal Republic of Germany as seen through the eyes of the young Britons visiting West Germany in the course of the Anglo-German youth exchanges.

0 85496 205 0   *Crown 8vo, 180 pp., illus., limp binding* £2.50

The Mass Media of the German Speaking Countries

by John Sandford

The first comprehensive introduction to the press and broadcasting systems in the Federal Republic of Germany, the GDR, Austria, German-speaking Switzerland, etc., with special emphasis on the development and present situation of the West German Press.

0 85496 203 4   *Demy 8vo, 235 pp., glossary, bibliography, index, cloth* £5.25

Weber in London, 1826

Edited by DAVID REYNOLDS

Selections from Carl Maria von Weber's letters and diary and from the writings of his contemporaries.

London, 1826, by Hermione Hobhouse

Weber 's Legacy, by John Warrack.

Profusely illustrated.

0 85496 403 7   20.9 × 26.7 *cm, 56 pp., oblong, illus., limp binding* £4.95

Of German Music

A SYMPOSIUM, *edited and introduced by* HANS-HUBERT SCHÖNZELER

From the early German organists to Hindemith and Schönberg, each chapter written by an expert on the period concerned.

0 85496 401 0   15.5 × 23.5 *cm. 328 pp., illus., bibliography, index, cloth* £6.50